YOUR BRILLIANT BONES and MARVELLOUS muscular system

FIND OUT HOW YOUR BODY WORKS!

Paul Mason

WAYLAND
www.waylandbooks.co.uk

CONTENTS

HUMAN BODY BASICS 3

YOUR BRILLIANT BONES AND MUSCLES.. 4

AN ENGINEERING MIRACLE 6

THE STAGGERING SPINE 8

BODY ARMOUR 10

BEND, DON'T BREAK 12

BONES FOR TRICKY JOBS 14

MARVELLOUS MUSCLES 16

MUSCLE POWER 18

MUSCLES OUT OF CONTROL! 20

FACING FACTS 22

BREAKING BONES 24

TEARS AND STRAINS 26

MAINTENANCE AND SERVICING 28

BONE AND MUSCLE WORDS 30

FOOD FOR BONES AND MUSCLES 31

INDEX 32

HUMAN BODY BASICS

Living things are grouped into a category called organisms. All organisms breathe, eat, excrete, grow, move, feel and reproduce. These are the seven 'life processes' that humans have in common with all living creatures, from sunflowers to snow leopards, crocodiles to crows.

Smallest parts

All organisms are made from tiny building blocks called cells. All cells have the same basic parts, but the exact structure of each cell depends on its job. Cells are so small that they can only be seen with a microscope.

Tissue and organs

Tissue is formed by lots of the same type of cell joining together. Types of tissue connect together to form organs. Different organs connect together in systems.

Body systems

Your body systems take care of different life processes. These include moving around, thinking, breathing, and digesting food.

skeletal muscle cells

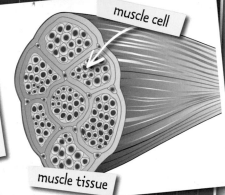

muscle cell

muscle tissue

Muscle cells join together in long strands called fibres. The fibres join together to form muscle tissue.

Muscle tissue can form muscles (organs), such as those in your arms and legs.

Your muscles work together to form your musculoskeletal system. This includes your bones and muscles — organs that help you move around.

YOUR BRILLIANT BONES AND MUSCLES

What's the reason you aren't blobbing around on the floor like a jellyfish right now? Your BONES! They provide a structure for your body – like a snail's shell, or a suit of armour, but on the inside. Bones and muscles give your body its shape.

Joining together

As a baby you had over 300 bones – but as you have grown, some of them have fused together. For example, your skull starts off as eight soft bony plates with gaps between them. There are good things and bad things about this arrangement:

Good things: it allows a baby's skull to compress in the narrow birth canal; after you're born, it also lets your skull expand as your brain grows.

Bad things: a flexible skull doesn't really provide very good brain protection.

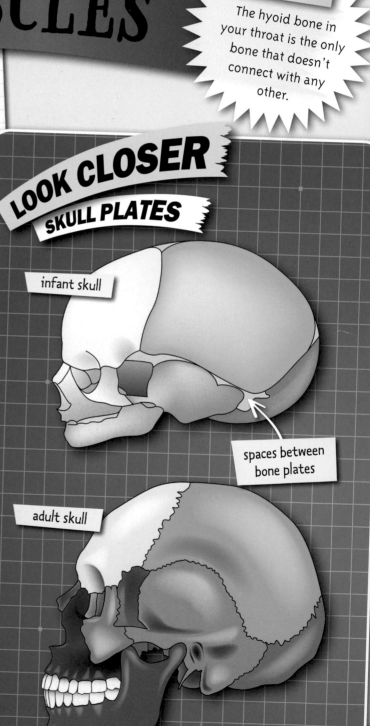

LOOK CLOSER
SKULL PLATES

infant skull

spaces between bone plates

adult skull

Soon after you were born, the bones in your skull started to join together. By the time you were about 18 months old, your skull had become a proper crash helmet (under your skin). As you grow, this kind of joining together happens only in some parts of the body. By the time you reach adulthood, your 300+ bones have become just 206.

Muscle magic

Of course, bones alone aren't much good. To stand up straight, sit and lie down, you also need muscles. These work like tug-of-war teams, pulling your bones to and fro as instructed by your brain.

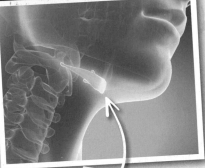

hyoid bone

The jaw muscle is very strong. You use it for everything from laughing to eating.

See for yourself

Test your muscle movement!

Hold your arm out straight with your palm up. Put your other hand on top, between the elbow and shoulder. It's now resting on your biceps muscle.

Next bend your arm, so that your fingertips touch your shoulder. The biceps muscle went from long to bunched-up, as it pulled your arm into a bent shape.

Bones are connected by joints. Muscles pull the bones on either side of the joints – which is what makes activities like running possible.

AN ENGINEERING MIRACLE

If your bones were made entirely of what most people THINK of as bone (the hard outer shell), it would be just about impossible to walk. Your legs would be so heavy that your muscles wouldn't be strong enough to move them!

BRILLIANT BODY FACT

Your smallest bone is deep in your ear, and is the size of a grain of rice.

LOOK CLOSER
INSIDE A BONE

This diagram shows a 'long bone' - one that is longer than it is wide.

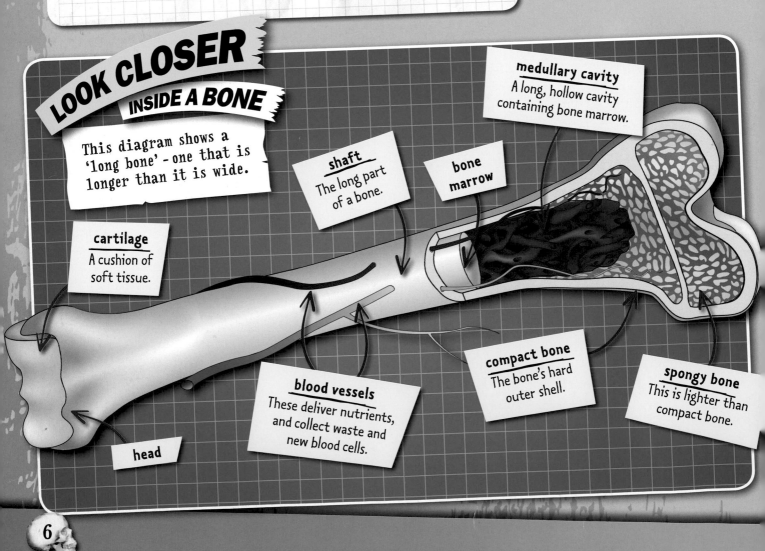

medullary cavity
A long, hollow cavity containing bone marrow.

shaft
The long part of a bone.

bone marrow

cartilage
A cushion of soft tissue.

blood vessels
These deliver nutrients, and collect waste and new blood cells.

compact bone
The bone's hard outer shell.

spongy bone
This is lighter than compact bone.

head

6

Light and strong

Bones contain some clever engineering that makes them lighter than you might expect. Only the outer parts are made of hard, heavy compact bone. The inner parts are lighter as they are made of spongy bone – a web of thin pieces of bone with spaces between them.

Inside your bones

The hollow cavity inside your bones is filled with bone marrow. This spongy, flexible substance is very important. In infants all bone marrow is red and produces red blood cells. In adults, only some bone marrow is red, most is yellow and serves as a fat store.

Bone types

Bones are named according to their shape. Those with a long middle section are called long bones. No surprise there. You also have four other types:

✱ **Flat bones** have wide, flat surfaces, like the ones that make up your skull and hips.

✱ **Short bones** are roughly as wide as they are long.

✱ **Sesamoid bones** are flat bones, such as your kneecap, that are held in place by a tendon (the end of a muscle).

✱ **Irregular bones** are oddly shaped bones that do not fit into any other category, such as the vertebrae in your back, or the mandible (lower jaw).

STRANGE BUT TRUE!

The largest bone in your body is your pelvis – though it's actually made of six bones that joined firmly together as you grew. Your longest bone is the femur in the thigh. It stretches for almost 25% of your total height.

pelvis

femur

This close-up view shows the hollow spaces inside spongy bone.

DID YOU KNOW?

Bone is stronger than some kinds of steel.

The outer layer of your bones – the layer known as compact bone – is REALLY tough. In fact, it's so tough that if you made an exact replica of a bone with an outer layer of steel, instead of compact bone, it wouldn't be as strong!

THE STAGGERING SPINE

That's staggering as in 'amazing', not staggering as in 'walking about looking as though you're about to fall down'. In fact, it's your spine that STOPS you from falling down. This amazing collection of bones is the most important in your body.

Protect and support

Your spine does two really big jobs. Firstly, it protects the spinal cord – a thick bundle of nerves that carries messages between the brain and the rest of your body. Without this, you cannot walk, kick a ball, swim or do anything physical. Secondly, your spine supports your upper body, from your bottom to the base of your skull. To do these two jobs it has to be both strong and flexible.

Your spine is amazingly flexible.

See for yourself

Find your spine!

Feel around behind you, to touch your backbone. You should be able to feel a series of little bony knobs. Each one is part of a vertebra.

You're not feeling the main part of the vertebrae. Each has three little spurs sticking out - two to the sides and one to the back. What you're feeling is the backward-pointing spur.

8

What's a spine made of?

A full-grown spine is made of a stack of 26 bones, called vertebrae. (A single one is called a vertebra.) Each vertebra has a hole in it for the spinal cord to pass through. The vertebrae are separated by soft pads called 'discs'.

Your spine is connected to over 100 different muscles, which allow it to bend in almost any direction. This structure allows the spine to be flexible, and protects the spinal cord.

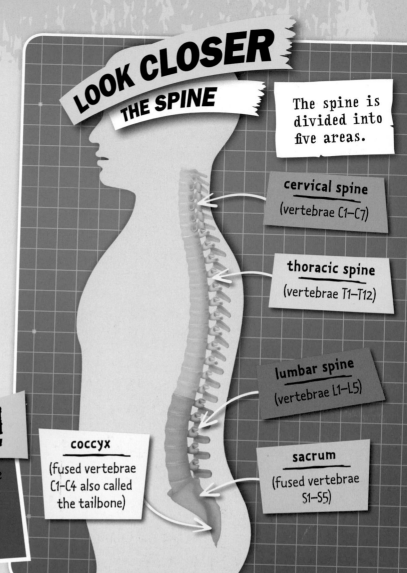

LOOK CLOSER
THE SPINE

The spine is divided into five areas.

cervical spine (vertebrae C1–C7)

thoracic spine (vertebrae T1–T12)

lumbar spine (vertebrae L1–L5)

coccyx (fused vertebrae C1–C4 also called the tailbone)

sacrum (fused vertebrae S1–S5)

STRANGE BUT TRUE!

When a baby is born it has 33 vertebrae in its spine. As it grows, some of them fuse together. A fully grown adult has 26 vertebrae in his or her spine.

Almost unbelievably, a giraffe's neck has the same number of bones as a human's. The giraffe's are a bit longer, though.

Some of a giraffe's neck vertebrae can be up to 25cm long!

DID YOU KNOW?

You're taller in the morning.

Together, the discs between your vertebrae make up over 25% of your spine's length. When you're upright, the discs are squashed down. They expand again when you lie down. The effect is that you are just a little shorter (about 1 cm in an adult) at the end of the day than at the beginning.

BODY ARMOUR

Most people, at some time, fall off a bike, tumble out of a tree, get crunched into while playing sports, or bang their head on a low doorway. So it's a good job that bones don't only work as a framework for your body. Some also work like a suit of armour, protecting vital organs from damage.

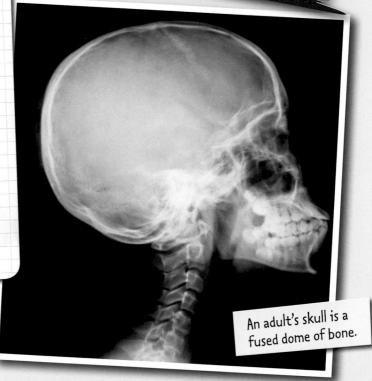

An adult's skull is a fused dome of bone.

Your body's helmet

Your skull protects your most important organ – your brain. It works a bit like a helmet under your skin, stopping anything from making contact with your brain and damaging it.

Of course, your skull has to be light enough for you to be able to move your head, so it can't be TOO thick. This is why it's a good idea to give it some backup, by wearing an actual helmet for things such as cycling, horse riding and skateboarding.

A protective cage

Your ribs form a layer of protection for important organs such as your heart and lungs, protecting them from damage. They wrap right around your upper body, protecting the front, sides and back.

Together, your ribs, sternum, and the top of your spine are called the ribcage. The top seven pairs are known as the true ribs and attach to the spine and to the sternum.

The next three pairs attach to the spine and to each other – they are called false ribs. At the bottom are the floating ribs, which attach to your spine only.

Rib bones are actually quite fragile. (You can damage a rib with a particularly violent sneeze!) They act like a car's crumple zone, breaking to absorb the force of a blow. Your ribs are joined together by muscles, which means that the ribcage is flexible and can expand when you breathe in.

STRANGE BUT TRUE!

In 2013, surgeons in the USA used a sheet of hard plastic to replace a section of someone's skull. The new skull section was an exact fit — it had been 3D printed using scans of the patient's head.

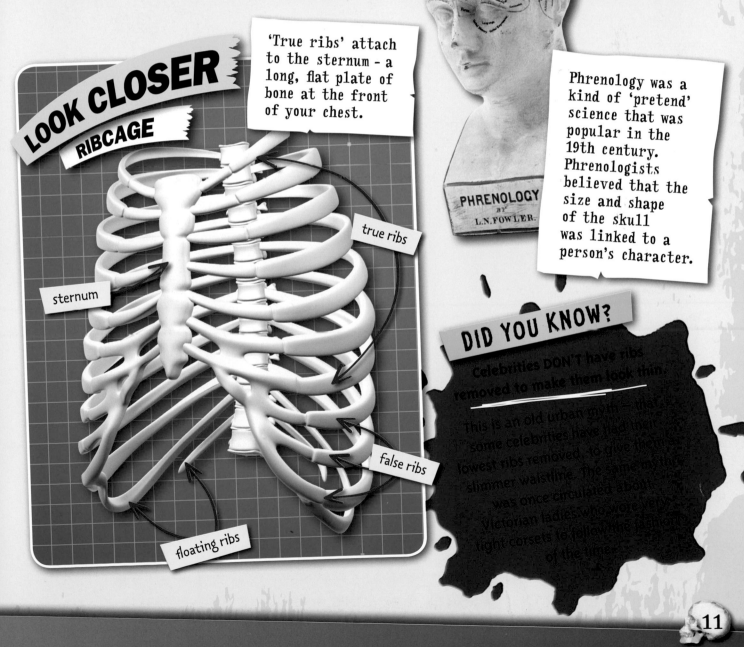

'True ribs' attach to the sternum - a long, flat plate of bone at the front of your chest.

LOOK CLOSER
RIBCAGE

sternum

true ribs

false ribs

floating ribs

PHRENOLOGY
BY
L.N. FOWLER.

Phrenology was a kind of 'pretend' science that was popular in the 19th century. Phrenologists believed that the size and shape of the skull was linked to a person's character.

DID YOU KNOW?

Celebrities DON'T have ribs removed to make them look thin.

This is an old urban myth — that some celebrities have had their lowest ribs removed, to give them a slimmer waistline. The same myth was once circulated about Victorian ladies who wore very tight corsets to follow the fashion of the time.

BEND, DON'T BREAK

If you bend a bone, it breaks. But humans, who are built of bone, have to bend all the time. Just think how tricky a forward roll or a cartwheel would be with a spine made of one long bone, instead of 26 smaller connected ones!

The skeleton

Your skeleton is made up of more than 200 separate bones. These all have to be connected, otherwise you would simply be a big heap of bones. The place where two or more bones meet is called a joint. To stop bones slipping and sliding apart you have ligaments. These hold your bones in place in the joint.

Moveable joints

Some joints cannot move at all, like those between the bony plates in your skull. Other joints allow a small amount of movement, like those between the bones in your spine (see pages 8–9). Many joints move freely, for example the ones at your wrist or ankle.

Types of joint

Your body has three main types of joint, named according to what they are made of.

✳ **Fibrous joints** are inflexible and hold together bones such as your skull plates, and the two bones in your forearm.

DID YOU KNOW?

Snake oil doesn't work!

In the 1800s, joint-pain medicines were known as 'snake oil'. They were said to make you as flexible as a snake. Salesmen even hired contortionists to show how effective their snake oil was!

Sadly, the medicines were rubbish.

* **Cartilaginous joints** bind bones together in a more flexible way than fibrous joints. For example, cartilaginous joints connect your ribs. That's why your ribcage can expand when you breathe in.

* **Synovial joints** are the most common kind of joint. Here, a fluid-filled sac separates two bones. The bones are often connected by ligaments – tough strands of fibre that hold the joint in position.

DON'T TRY THIS AT HOME!

'Major Zamora' was a well-known contortionist in the USA during the early 1900s. Zamora was only 81cm tall, and weighed just 24kg, but he was also incredibly flexible. He could get through tiny holes — his most famous trick was squeezing himself into a large bottle, then climbing out again.

LOOK CLOSER
SYNOVIAL JOINT

cartilage pad at end of bone

ligament

synovial sac

bone

synovial fluid

tendon

A synovial joint, the most common type in the human body.

Contortionists, like the two girls here, have often trained since they were small children.

BONES FOR TRICKY JOBS

Think about your arm. It has a simple job – all it has to do is bend at the elbow. So the bones in your arm are simple: just one main bone in your upper arm and two in your lower arm. Now think about the hundreds of jobs your hands and feet do. No wonder they contain a lot of bones!

Hands and feet

Your hands and feet are used for really delicate jobs: playing the guitar, dancing, stroking the cat, passing a football, and so on. Imagine trying to play the guitar if your fingers only contained one long, straight bone – impossible! Fortunately, each of your hands contains 27 bones, and each foot has just one fewer, at 26.

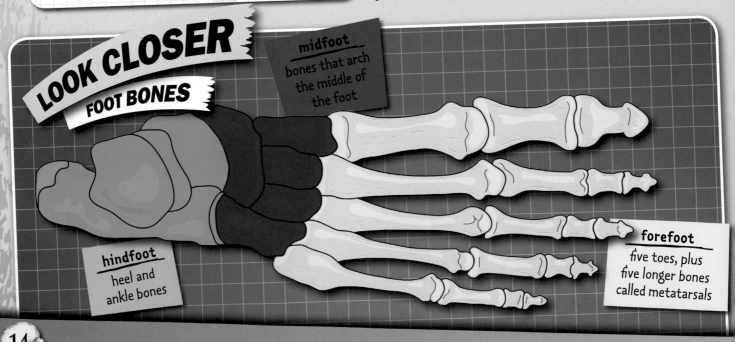

LOOK CLOSER
FOOT BONES

midfoot
bones that arch the middle of the foot

hindfoot
heel and ankle bones

forefoot
five toes, plus five longer bones called metatarsals

Muscle-free hands

Bones are moved by muscles, which are usually located nearby. If your fingers contained muscles, though, each one would be as big as a sausage. So, amazingly, there are NO muscles in your fingers. Instead, the tendons in your fingers are connected to muscles in the palms of your hands and your forearm.

Multi-purpose feet

Your feet allow you to balance, which is essential for all sorts of actions – simply walking or running, as well for dancing, gymnastics, or just pedalling your bike. As a result, feet are almost as complicated as hands. They have just one bone fewer per foot – plus 33 joints, 107 ligaments and 19 muscles.

LOOK CLOSER
TENDONS IN THE HAND

Small muscles allow fine movement.

Tendons stretching from the inside forearm muscles bend the lower part of the fingers.

Tendons from muscles in the outside forearm allow the hand to open up.

See for yourself

Some fingers share tendons with their next-door neighbours. Try this experiment as a demonstration:

Hold your hand out with the palm facing you. Now bend your little finger. Is it the only one that moves? Do the same experiment with your other fingers and your thumb. Can you move any fingers without one of the others moving too?

STRANGE BUT TRUE!

As this X-ray shows, not everyone is born with 10 fingers and 10 toes. Having more than the usual number is called polydactylism.

MARVELLOUS MUSCLES

If you didn't have muscles, you couldn't turn a page of this book. You also couldn't eat, breathe, sneeze, flick your older brother's ear, or run away. In fact, you couldn't make ANY of the millions of movements you make every day. Without muscles, you would literally be going nowhere!

and pulls, the other muscle stays relaxed. Then, to move the joint in the other direction, the muscles change jobs. The first muscle relaxes, while the second one shortens itself and pulls.

Types of muscle

The muscles you use to move around are called skeletal muscles. Your body also comes equipped with two other types – smooth muscle and cardiac muscle. You can find out more about these on page 21.

Working in pairs

Most skeletal muscles are attached to bones on either side of a joint (see pages 12 and 13). Each joint has a pair of muscles. While one muscle in the pair shortens itself (contracts)

LOOK CLOSER
MOVING MUSCLES

When one muscle is contracting (pulling), the opposite muscle is relaxed.

The biceps muscle contracts and shortens to bend the arm.

The triceps muscle is relaxed and long.

The biceps muscle lengthens as it relaxes.

The triceps muscle contracts slightly to straighten the arm.

What is a muscle made of?

Skeletal muscles are made of long tubes called fascicles. Inside each fascicle are long muscle fibres. These are separated into slow-twitch and fast-twitch fibres, depending on how quickly they can contract. Fast-twitch muscles are used for short bursts of activity, such as a sprint, while slow-twitch are used for longer, slower activity, such as walking.

✳ **Fast-twitch** muscles contract very quickly. They do not need oxygen, but they run out of energy very quickly.

✳ **Slow-twitch** muscle fibres do not contract quickly, but keep working for a long time. They make energy using oxygen and food obtained from your blood.

LOOK CLOSER
INSIDE A MUSCLE

muscle

bone

muscle fibre made of muscle cells

fascicle

tendon

See for yourself

Next time you eat a chicken, have a look at the different colours of the meat.

✳ **The dark leg meat** is slow-twitch muscle, used for low-energy walking around. Its dark colour comes from the blood supply needed by slow-twitch muscles.

✳ **White breast meat** is mostly fast-twitch muscle, designed to power the wings in high-energy bursts. It does not need oxygen for energy, and contains fewer blood vessels.

DID YOU KNOW?

Your biggest muscle is behind you.

It is in your bottom and is called the gluteus maximus. It helps to move your hips and thighs when you walk.

The smallest muscle in the body is inside your ear — it is just 1.25mm long!

MUSCLE POWER

Each year a competition is held to decide the 'World's Strongest Man'. Contestants compete in events from lifting concrete balls to pulling amazingly heavy trucks. But how do they make their muscles so strong?

Amazing muscles

We all develop our muscle power and size as we grow. The more you use your muscles the more toned and strong they will become. This means that everyday tasks are easier and also that you develop endurance – the ability to keep going longer before you tire. For muscles to become even stronger, they need to be used even more.

How do muscles grow?

Muscles grow larger by being used. When you use a muscle, it damages the muscle fibres. Harder use results in more damage. When the body repairs the damaged muscles, it makes them larger. It's the body's way of preparing the muscles, in case they are asked to produce more power again.

Powerful muscles

The most powerful muscle in your body is your jaw muscle. The tongue would be a contender – but it actually contains eight muscles, so is disqualified.

Your most over-powered muscles are the muscles of your eye. These are about 100 times stronger than they really need to be for moving a lightweight eyeball around.

Six pairs of muscles work together to move the eyes in almost any direction.

Cramp!

Sometimes, your muscles suddenly tighten up, without you asking them to. It can be very painful! We call this painful tightening 'cramp'. It usually happens while people are doing exercise, but you can also get cramp after exercise, especially if your muscles have been working hard. The best way to get rid of it is by gently stretching the muscle out, and rubbing it to help it relax.

Cramp is often linked with doing too much exercise when the muscle's oxygen supply is low or through not drinking enough fluid.

DID YOU KNOW?

You can't grow new muscles.

Humans are born with all the muscle fibres they will ever have, so you cannot grow new muscle fibres. What CAN happen is that each fibre in a muscle grows thicker and longer. This happens when the muscles are used — which is why working out at the gym makes your muscles larger.

STRANGE BUT TRUE!

In 1957, an American weightlifter called Paul Anderson decided to show just how powerful his muscles were. He loaded up a table with car parts and a safe full of lead — then lifted it up! It seems to have weighed 2,844kg* — the greatest weight ever lifted by a human, before or since.

*that's nearly three medium-sized great white sharks!

MUSCLES OUT OF CONTROL!

Have you ever stayed too long in cold water, or ignored your mum when she told you to put on a coat before going out? If so, you have probably ended up with your teeth chattering and your whole body shaking. Which proves you can't always control your muscles – sometimes, your body just takes over.

What makes you shiver?

Shivering is a reflex – something your body does automatically in response to a situation. In this case, it's a response to getting cold. Your body knows that when you use muscles, they warm up and give off heat.

In this image, red = hot, blue = cold. You can see how much heat the weightlifter's arms are releasing!

So the central nervous system sends an automatic signal to muscles all over your body, telling them to contract many times really quickly.

Other common reflex actions

Shivering is just one of the muscle movements we don't control. Other reflex actions include:

* **ducking** if something is thrown towards your head

* **quickly lifting your foot** if you step on something sharp

* **jerking back** if you accidentally touch something hot.

These are all examples of your central nervous system taking over control of your skeletal muscles. Normally you control these yourself. In an emergency, the nervous system steps in.

Smooth and cardiac muscles

As well as skeletal muscles, you have smooth and cardiac (heart) muscles. Smooth muscle makes up many of your internal organs, such as your lungs and stomach. These are muscles you NEVER have to think about controlling. This is a good job, too – imagine having to remind your heart to beat, your stomach to process food, or your lungs to breathe every single time!

smooth muscle cells

Many organs in the digestive system are made of smooth muscle.

Muscles contract and relax to move food through the gut.

STRANGE BUT TRUE!

Babies are born with 'primitive reflexes', which disappear as they grow. One of these is the grasp reflex. Touching a baby's hand will cause it to curl around in a tight grasp. This reflex disappears when the baby is 4–6 months old.

The cells of heart muscle are Y-shaped. Each tip links to another cell, making the network of cells very strong.

DID YOU KNOW?

One muscle never stops working.

Your heart is the hardest-working muscle in your body. It never stops. When you are resting, a healthy heart beats between 50 and 90 times per minute on average. Usually a child's heart beats faster than an adult's.

FACING FACTS

You have more than 40 muscles in your face. Without them, life would be very dull – you could not eat, speak, or show your feelings. Just try looking surprised, or cross, without moving any part of your face!

Emotional muscles

How can you tell what someone else is feeling? By looking at their face. Your face contains the most complex set of muscles in your body, and allows you to show your emotions. Frowning, laughing, crying, looking down your nose at people – these are all messages about how you're feeling. We make most of these emotional muscle movements automatically, without thinking about them.

Practical muscles

Of course, the muscles in your face have practical jobs to do. They allow you to chew your food, sniff the air, talk, drink, blink, and look around. This is why the temporomandibular joint (the one that joins your jaw to your skull) is one of the most complicated in the body. It has to be able to move in all directions.

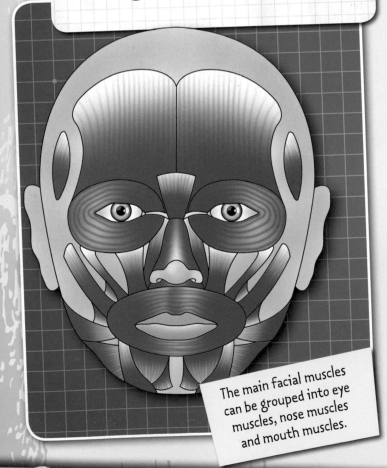

The main facial muscles can be grouped into eye muscles, nose muscles and mouth muscles.

temporomandibular joint

Here are our top four clues that someone may not be being absolutely honest:

① **False facial expressions are usually asymmetrical.**

So, for example, if someone smiles with only one side of their face, they probably aren't really happy.

② **It is almost impossible to control the muscles around your eyes.**

It is easy to make your mouth into a smiling shape - but tricky to make your eyes crinkle up convincingly, unless you REALLY feel happy or amused.

③ **Most people hide other emotions behind a smile.**

If you spot someone giving you a false smile, it's usually because they are trying to hide a different emotion. Ask yourself what it might be!

④ **Sad chins reveal a faker.**

Nine out of 10 people find it impossible to deliberately lower the corners of their mouth and look sad without using their chin muscles. People who are REALLY sad don't do this. So if you see the chin muscles move, the 'sad' person is probably faking it.

See for yourself

Read the **Did you know?** panel then test the clues on a friend. Eventually, with practice, they might be able to fake it convincingly.

If this happens, remember - someone who has got away with being dishonest will NOT be able to stop a split-second look of triumph.

BREAKING BONES

Your body has ways of mending itself and can make repairs to almost any body part that gets broken or damaged. In fact, some of the only body parts that cannot be fixed are your teeth. If you break or damage your second teeth, there is nothing your body can do (but a dentist CAN fix them).

Keeping straight

Some bone breaks cause the bones to go out of line. To mend properly they need to be kept straight. Doctors take an X-ray to see what position the bones are in so that they can then move them into a straight position. To keep them straight, and to stop them moving, you normally have to wear a plaster cast until the break has mended.

How do bones mend?

When you break a bone your body is quick to respond. First, it produces lots of new cells and blood vessels at the site of the break. The new cells build up on the broken bone, like a bridge being built out from a riverbank. Eventually, they meet new cells that have been growing from the other side of the break, and the bone is healed.

Fractured bones usually mend in one to two months, though it depends on how serious the fracture was.

DID YOU KNOW?

Some saws won't cut.

When you break a bone, you often have to wear a plaster cast. Later, the plaster cast is cut off with a whirring saw. The weird thing is, the worst the saw can do is tickle you.

This is because the saw works by vibrating against the hard cast. Once it touches skin, the skin (which isn't hard) just vibrates up and down with the saw. It tickles, but it doesn't cut.

LOOK CLOSER
MENDING BONES

Broken bones can heal themselves. How long it takes will depend on how bad the break is.

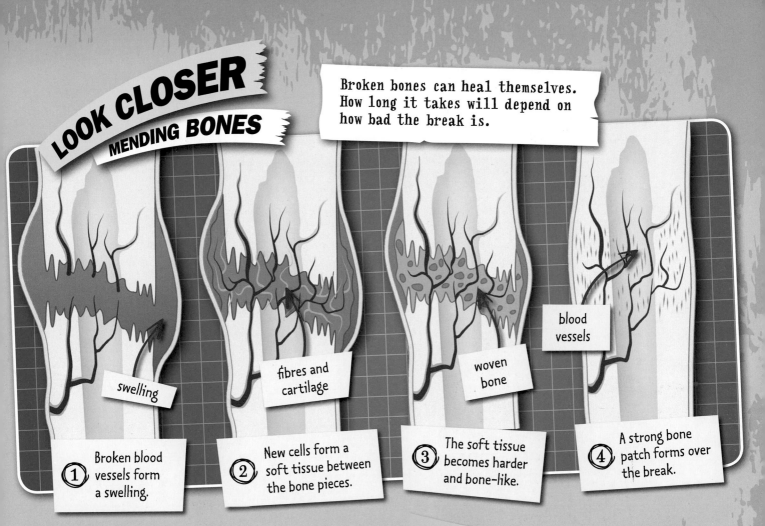

swelling

fibres and cartilage

woven bone

blood vessels

① Broken blood vessels form a swelling.

② New cells form a soft tissue between the bone pieces.

③ The soft tissue becomes harder and bone-like.

④ A strong bone patch forms over the break.

DON'T TRY THIS AT HOME!

Sandals were the footwear of choice in Ancient Egypt, but these were EXTREMELY difficult to walk in if you had lost your big toe.

Fortunately, the Ancient Egyptians developed the world's first functional prosthetic bone. It was an artificial big toe, and was designed to make it possible to wear sandals if you had lost your big toe in an accident.

STRANGE BUT TRUE!

Arms are among the bones adults break most often, making up almost half of the total number. Among children, the collarbone is the most commonly broken bone.

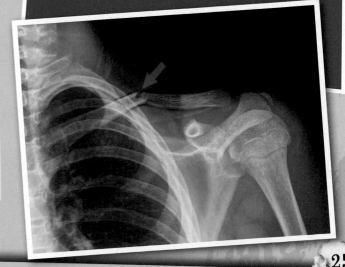

TEARS AND STRAINS

Have you ever watched track athletics, football, or any other sport where people run fast? If so, you have probably seen someone suddenly *stop* running fast and clutch the back of their leg. The commentator might say something like, 'He/she has torn a muscle.' So, just what is a torn muscle?

Injury time

A torn muscle is a muscle that has been pulled apart, partly or completely. Other common injuries include damaging the tendons at the ends of a muscle, or the ligaments of a joint. Usually the body can heal itself or adapt, but for serious injuries an operation may be needed to repair the damage.

Torn muscles

Muscles get torn for many reasons. The most common are doing sudden, hard activity, such as picking up a heavy weight, without warming up (see page 29). Muscles also sometimes tear because they have been stretched too far, for example when one of your feet skids and you do the splits.

Snapping tendons

Tendons join muscles to bones. In younger people, tendons are very strong. Their muscles usually tear before one of the tendons breaks. As people get older, though, their tendons weaken. It becomes more likely that their tendon will break, rather than the muscle tearing.

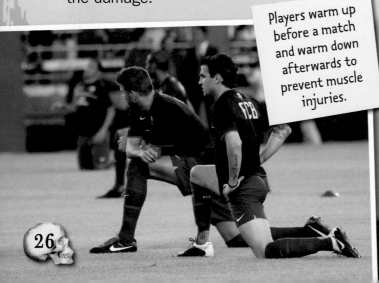

Players warm up before a match and warm down afterwards to prevent muscle injuries.

STRANGE BUT TRUE!

The palmaris longus is the tendon crabs use to open and close their claws. Unless you have claws, you don't really need one.

LOOK CLOSER
TOUGH TENDONS

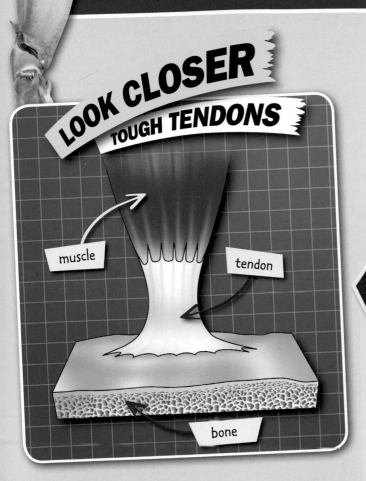

muscle

tendon

bone

Tearing ligaments

Ligaments are strips of tough fibre that hold joints in place. If the joint is forced out of position, like when you step on something and twist your ankle, the ligaments can be damaged or torn completely. The joints most often affected by ligament damage are the knees and ankles.

See for yourself

Your wrist might contain a tendon called the palmaris longus...

Only about 14% of people do not have this tendon. To check if you do:

① Touch the tips of your little finger and thumb together

② Bend your wrist towards you.

If you have a palmaris longus, you will be able to see the tendon clearly, sticking up along the centre of your wrist.

DON'T TRY THIS AT HOME!

An Ancient Greek myth tells of Achilles' heel. Achilles' mum was told that he would one day be killed in battle. She didn't like this idea, so dunked him into a magical river. This made his body like armour — apart from his heel, which she had held onto during the dunking. Years later, Achilles was busy attacking the city of Troy when a poisoned arrow hit his heel. Achilles died. Today, the tendon in your heel is named the Achilles tendon in his memory.

MAINTENANCE AND SERVICING

Your bones are continuously being broken down and replaced. After about seven years, none of the original bone is left – you have a new one! However, after the age of about 30 your bone production slows down. More bone is broken down than is made, which is why fractures are more common among the elderly.

Boosting your bones

Fortunately, there is some good news. By building strong bones when you are young, you can can delay your bones' disappearing act. So, how do you go about it?

① Think (and drink) calcium

Calcium is an important mineral for building bone. It also helps your muscles to function and keeps your heart beating efficiently. Your body gets calcium from milk and cheese, green-leaf vegetables, soya beans, nuts, and fish such as sardines, where you eat the bones.

② Back up the vitamin D

Your body uses vitamin D to turn calcium into bone. You can eat it in prawns, sardines (again), egg yolks or tuna fish. Or you can just get 15 minutes of sunshine every other day – which stimulates your body to produce vitamin D.

Your body can get calcium from milk.

Sunlight helps you produce vitamin D.

③ Exercise

Bones (and muscles) get stronger if they need to get stronger. If you sit around playing video games all day, your body doesn't waste energy making your bones strong. If you go out for a run, skateboard, do gymnastics, play football, or do any other exercise that puts weight on your bones, they will grow stronger.

Exercise strengthens your muscles and bones.

Stretches are an important part of exercise!

Marvellous muscles

Like bones, muscles need to be used. This doesn't mean you have to go to the gym every day – but if you do not make your muscles work, they become smaller and less fit. Always warm up before working your muscles, to prevent tears and strains. Start them moving gently, to warn them that some harder exercise is coming. Remember to warm down after exercise too – this helps to prevent muscle damage.

STRANGE BUT TRUE!

It's worth looking after your bones and muscles: they might have to last you a long time. One of the world's oldest people was Jeanne Calment of France, who lived to be 122 years, 164 days.

Calment was said to have been in perfect health for most of her life. She even took up fencing when she was 85. Calment only began to feel old when she broke her leg – at the age of 114.

Jean Calment

BONE AND MUSCLE WORDS

central nervous system the brain and spinal cord

compact bone the hard, dense substance that makes up the outer shell of a bone

contortionist a person who is able to bend their body into extreme, unusual shapes

contract to become shorter and tighter

flexible bendable, or able to move in a lot of different ways

fragile easily broken

fused permanently joined together

joint a connection between one bone and another

ligament a fibre that supports the joints of bones, holding them in position

organ part of a living creature that has a particular function. Your heart is an organ, for example, and its function is to pump blood around your body.

pelvis the bony structure that supports the spine, and has the legs attached to it (at the hips)

plaster cast a hard, light, tube-like case that is built around an arm or leg with a broken bone to protect the bone while it heals

prosthetic having to do with an artificial body part. An artificial leg, for example, is also called a prosthetic leg.

reflex an automatic response that happens without you thinking about it

scan an image showing what is going on inside someone's body

skeletal muscle a muscle used for movement, which can be voluntarily controlled

smooth muscle muscle tissue that makes up involuntary muscles, such as those in your digestive system

spinal cord the thick bundle of nerves that carries messages from your brain to the rest of your body and controls body movements

spur something that sticks out from the main part of an object, such as the three bony knobs that stick out from each vertebra

sternum a long, flat plate of bone in the centre of your chest, to which some of your ribs are attached

tendon the end of a muscle that connects the muscle to a bone

urban myth a story that is told as though it is true, even though it seems unlikely (and is not true)

vertebra a bone in the spine, or backbone. The plural of vertebra is vertebrae.

warm up to prepare for exercise by doing some gentle activity

FOOD FOR BONES
AND MUSCLES

Are you hungry for extra information about bones and muscles? Here are some good places to find out more:

BOOKS TO READ

Truth or Busted: *The Fact or Fiction Behind Human Bodies,* Paul Mason, Wayland 2014

Go Figure: *A Maths Journey Through the Human Body,* Anne Rooney, Wayland 2014

MindWebs: *Human Body,*
Anna Claybourne, Wayland 2014

The World in Infographics: *The Human Body,* Jon Richards and Ed Simkins, Wayland 2013

WEBSITES

http://kidshealth.org/kid/htbw/bones.html
http://kidshealth.org/kid/htbw/muscles.html

This website is a really good place to find out all sorts of information about the human body. It has excellent sections on muscles and bones.

http://www.childrensuniversity.manchester. ac.uk/interactives/science/exercise//

The Children's University of Manchester, UK, has all sorts of information for kids, presented in the form of labelled illustrations. It includes a section on exercise from which you can move on to information about muscles and the heart.

PLACES TO VISIT

In London, the **Science Museum** has regular exhibitions and displays explaining how the body works. The museum is at:

Exhibition Road
South Kensington
London SW7 2DD

The **Science Museum** also has a really good website:

http://www.sciencemuseum.org.uk/WhoAmI/ FindOutMore/Yourbody.aspx

The **Natural History Museum** has an amazing 'Human Biology Gallery' where you can find out how the human skeleton has influenced man-made structures. The museum is at:

The Natural History Museum
Cromwell Road
London SW7 5BD

The museum also has a good website:

http://www.nhm.ac.uk/visit-us/galleries/blue-zone/human-biology/

INDEX

animals 3, 4, 9, 27

biceps 5, 16
blood 6, 7, 17, 24, 25
bones 3, 4, 6–7, 8–9, 10–11, 12, 13,
    14–15, 17, 24–25, 26, 27, 28, 29
    breaking 24–25, 28, 29
    number of 4, 5, 7, 9, 12, 14, 15
    shape 6, 7
    size 6
bone marrow 6, 7, 25
breathing 3, 13, 16

calcium 28
cardiac muscle 16, 21
cartilage 6, 12, 13, 25
cells 3, 6, 7, 17, 21, 24, 25
central nervous system 20, 21, 30
collarbone 25
compact bone 6, 7
contortionists 12, 13, 26, 30
cramp 19

diet 28–29
digestive system 3, 21

exercise 19, 26, 29
eyes 18, 22, 23

face 22–23
fascicles 17
feet 14, 15, 20, 25
femur 7

gluteus maximus 17
growing 3, 4, 5, 9, 18

hands 14, 15
heart 20, 21, 26
hyoid bone 4, 5

jaw 5, 7, 18, 22
joints 5, 12–13, 15, 16, 22, 26,
    27, 30

knee 7, 27

ligaments 12, 13, 15, 26, 27, 30
lungs 21

moving 3, 5, 8, 12, 15, 16, 17,
    22, 23, 29
muscles 3, 4, 5, 6, 7, 11, 15, 16–17,
    18–19, 20–21, 22–23, 26, 28, 29
    damage 18, 26–27, 29
    number of 9, 15, 16, 18, 22
    pairs 16, 18
    size 15, 17, 18, 19, 29
    strength 5, 6, 18–19, 29
    types 16, 17

muscle fibres 3, 13, 17, 18, 19, 25

pelvis 7, 30
phrenology 11
polydactylism 15
prosthetics 25, 30

reflexes 20–21, 30
ribs 10–11, 13

skeleton 12
skull 4, 5, 7, 8, 10, 11, 12, 22
smooth muscle 16, 21, 30
spine 8–9, 10, 11, 12
spongy bone 6, 7
sternum 10, 11, 30

tendons 7, 13, 15, 26, 27, 30
tongue 5, 18
triceps 16

vertebrae 7, 8, 9, 30
vitamin D 28

X–rays 15, 24

WAYLAND

First published in Great Britain
in 2015 by Wayland
Copyright © Wayland, 2015
All rights reserved.

Editor: Annabel Stones
Designer: Rocket Design (East Anglia) Ltd
Consultant: John Clancy, Former Senior
Lecturer in Applied Human Physiology
Proofreader: Susie Brooks

Dewey Number: 612.1-dc23
ISBN: 978 0 7502 92467
Library ebook ISBN: 978 0 7502 92474

10 9 8 7 6 5 4 3 2 1

Wayland, an imprint of
Hachette Children's Group
Part of Hodder & Stoughton
Carmelite House
50 Victoria Embankment
London EC4Y 0DZ

An Hachette UK Company
www.hachette.co.uk
www.hachettechildrens.co.uk
Printed in China

Artwork: Stefan Chabluk: p3 t, p3
cr, p4, p13 l, p15 t, p17 c, p25 t;
Ian Thompson: p3 cl, p16, p22 l,
p27 cl.

Picture credits: Getty Images: p11 cr Stephen Oliver,
p19 tr Keystone / Stringer, p22 br Sciepro, p25 bl
DEA / G DAGLI ORTI, p29 br Ian Cook / Contributor;
Science Photo Library: p15 br SOVEREIGN, ISM,
p20 TED KINSMAN; Shutterstock: Cover, p3 b, p5
cl, p5 cr, p5 br, p6, p7 c, p7 r, p7 bl, p8 l, p8 r, p9 t,
p9 b, p10, p11 l, p12, p13 r, p14 tl, p14 b, p17 br,
p18 tl, p18 br, p19 cl, p19 br, p21 tr, p21 bl, p21
br, p23 all, p24, p25 br, p26 Natursports,
p27 tl, p27 br, p28 bl, p28 br, p29 tr, p29 cl.
Graphic elements from Shutterstock.

The website addresses (URLs) included in this book
were valid at the time of going to press. However,
it is possible that contents or addresses may have
changed since the publication of this book. No
responsibility for any such changes can be accepted
by either the author or the Publisher

Every effort has been made to clear copyright.
Should there be any inadvertent omission, please
apply to the publisher for rectification.

YOUR BRILLIANT BODY

Marvel at the wonders of the human body with this fact-packed series.

978 0 7502 9388 4

978 0 7502 9246 7

978 0 7502 9240 5

978 0 7502 9237 5

978 0 7502 9249 8

978 0 7502 9243 6

Find out more about the human body with other Wayland titles:

978 0 7502 7868 3

978 0 7502 8158 4

978 0 7502 8241 3

978 0 7502 8280 2

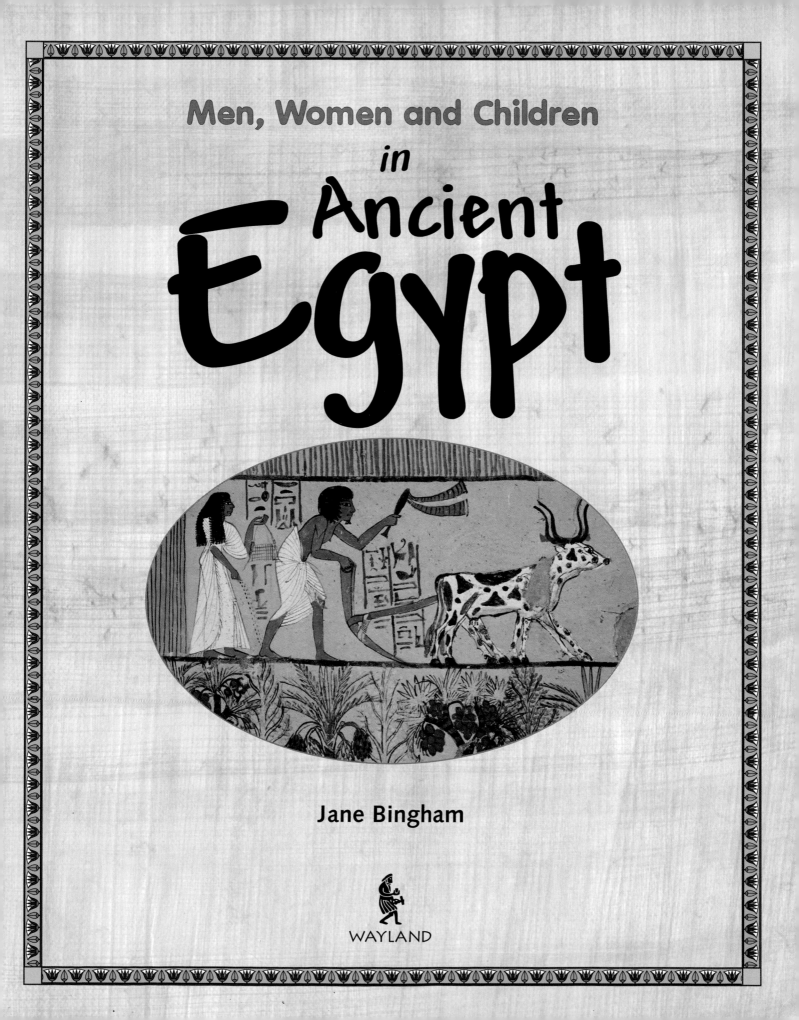

Men, Women and Children

in

Ancient Egypt

Jane Bingham

WAYLAND

First published in 2007 by Wayland, a division of Hachette Children's Books, an Hachette Livre UK company.
Copyright © Wayland 2007

Wayland, 338 Euston Road, London NW1 3BH

Wayland Australia, Hachette Children's Books
Level 17/207 Kent Street
Sydney, NSW 2000

British Library Cataloguing in
Publication Data
Bingham, Jane
  Ancient Egypt. - (Men, women and children)
  1. Egypt - Social life and customs - To 322 B.C. - Juvenile literature
  2. Egypt - Social conditions - Juvenile literature
  I. Title
  932

ISBN: 978-0-7502-5076-4

Printed in China

Cover (main image): Queen Nefertiti was the chief wife of Pharaoh Akhaten and the mother of six daughters. Here she wears a simple crown and a wide bead necklace.

Picture acknowledgments: ARPL/HIP/Topfoto: 11; The Art Archive/Corbis: 3, 18; Bettmann/Corbis: 7; The British Library/HIP/Topfoto: 10, 14; The British Museum/Werner Forman Archive: 19; The British Museum/HIP/Topfoto: front cover tl & bl, 5, 13, 15, 24, 25; The Egyptian Museum, Cairo/Werner Forman Archive: 16; Werner Forman Archive: 26; Werner Forman Archive/Corbis: 12; Historical Picture Archive/Corbis: 22; Gianni Dagli Orti/Corbis: 17; Ronald Sheridan/AAAC: 20; Spectrum Colour Library/HIP/Topfoto:front cover cl, 9; Topfoto: 27; Charles Walker/Topfoto: front cover main, 23; Ron Watts/Corbis: 21; Roger Wood/Corbis: 8.

Map by Peter Bull.

CONTENTS

WHO WERE THE ANCIENT EGYPTIANS? 6

EGYPTIAN MEN, WOMEN AND CHILDREN 8

WHO WAS IN CHARGE IN ANCIENT EGYPTIAN TIMES? 10

WHAT WAS LIFE LIKE IN AN EGYPTIAN FAMILY? 12

DID EGYPTIAN CHILDREN GO TO SCHOOL? 16

WHAT JOBS DID EGYPTIAN PEOPLE DO? 18

WHAT DID EGYPTIAN ADULTS AND CHILDREN WEAR? 22

HOW DID EGYPTIAN ADULTS AND CHILDREN HAVE FUN? 24

HOW IMPORTANT WAS RELIGION FOR THE EGYPTIANS? 26

GLOSSARY 28

FURTHER INFORMATION 29

INDEX 30

Words that appear in **bold**
can be found in the glossary
on page 28.

WHO WERE THE ANCIENT EGYPTIANS?

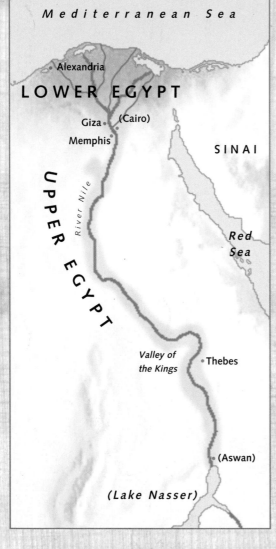

▲ A map of Ancient Egypt, showing the main cities. (Modern names are shown in brackets.)

The Ancient Egyptians began as a race of people living on the banks of the River Nile, in North Africa. Gradually, they learnt how to grow crops and **irrigate** the land, and, by 5000 BC, they were farming the **fertile** soil beside the river. The farmers settled in villages which, over time, grew into larger communities.

EGYPT UNITES

By the 4th century BC, there were two kingdoms on the River Nile: Upper Egypt and Lower Egypt. Then, around 3100 BC, the kingdoms were united by **Pharaoh** Menes. He built a capital city at Memphis, and started a **dynasty** (or family) of powerful rulers.

THREE PERIODS

The Ancient Egyptian **civilization** lasted for over 2000 years. Historians have identified three great periods in this long history. The Old Kingdom (c.2575 –2150 BC) was the time when most of the great pyramids were built. The Middle Kingdom (c.1975-1640 BC) was the period when art and literature flourished. The New Kingdom (c.1539-1075 BC) was a time of expansion, when the Egyptians gained an empire that was at its largest in about 1450 BC.

EYGPTIAN TIMELINE

5000 BC   4000   3000

c.5000 BC Farming begins in the Nile valley.

c.3100 BC Pharaoh Menes unites Upper and Lower Egypt.

c.2575 BC Old Kingdom begins.

THE END OF THE EMPIRE

By the 1st century BC, the Egyptian Empire had started to weaken and the Egyptians had to defend themselves against many enemies. Finally, in 332 BC, they were conquered by a Greek army led by Alexander the Great. For the next 300 years, Egypt was ruled by members of the Ptolemy family, who were descended from one of Alexander's **generals**.

In 32 BC, Rome went to war with Egypt. The Egyptians were defeated and their ruler, Queen Cleopatra, killed herself. Egypt became part of the Roman Empire in 30 BC, and the great Egyptian civilization came to an end.

REAL LIVES

CLEOPATRA: THE LAST QUEEN OF EGYPT

Cleopatra (shown here) was joint ruler of Egypt, first with her father and later with her husband. After her husband died, she ruled on her own. She fell in love with a Roman general, Mark Anthony. They combined their armies to fight against the Romans, but they were defeated and Cleopatra committed suicide. Historians believe that she killed herself by applying a poisonous snake to her arm.

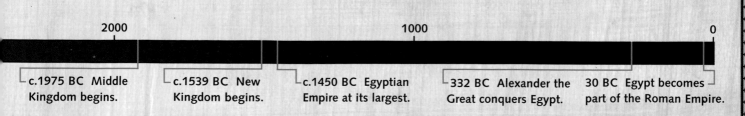

| 2000 | 1000 | 0 |

c.1975 BC Middle Kingdom begins.

c.1539 BC New Kingdom begins.

c.1450 BC Egyptian Empire at its largest.

332 BC Alexander the Great conquers Egypt.

30 BC Egypt becomes part of the Roman Empire.

EGYPTIAN MEN, WOMEN AND CHILDREN

Ancient Egyptian society was divided into two main classes: the wealthy rulers and nobles, and the ordinary working people. Men of all classes had more freedom than women, but Egyptian women had more rights than women in Ancient Greece or Rome.

EGYPTIAN MEN

Egyptian men saw themselves as the head of the household, but most of them left the job of running the home to their wives. By law, men could have as many wives as they wished, and some pharaohs had hundreds. However, most Egyptians could only afford to support one wife.

EGYPTIAN WOMEN

Women in Ancient Egypt had the right to own property and to run a business. If an Egyptian woman was accused of a crime, she could appear in court to defend herself.

Wealthy women had a large staff of servants to help them run their homes, but women from poor families did all the housework themselves, with the help of their daughters. Only a few noblewomen went out to work but poorer women often helped their husbands in the fields, or did other jobs in the community (see pages 18-21). Egyptian women of all classes were kept very busy bringing up their

▲ The most important person in Ancient Egypt was the pharaoh, or king. Ancient Egyptian pharaohs were treated like gods by their people. This painting shows Pharaoh Ramses III embracing the goddess Isis.

families. It was not unusual for a woman to give birth to ten children, although it was rare for all the children to survive.

EGYPTIAN CHILDREN

Children were greatly valued in Egyptian society and most children enjoyed a close family life. However, by the time they were 12 years old, Egyptian children were seen as adults. Girls could be married at this age, and the children from poorer families were expected to start full time work. Some Egyptian children started to work with their parents before they were even five years old.

◄ An Egyptian carving of a husband and wife. The couple seem to be fond of each other, as the wife has her arm around her husband's shoulders. The two small figures are probably their children.

REAL LIVES

NAUNAKTE: A NOBLEWOMAN

An Egyptian noblewoman, known simply as Lady Naunakte, wrote a will before she died. Naunakte clearly had property and wealth of her own, independently of her husband. In her will, she proudly announced that she had managed to provide for all her children. Naunakte wrote "I am a free woman of Egypt. I have raised eight children, and have provided them with everything suitable for their station in life."

WHO WAS IN CHARGE IN ANCIENT EGYPTIAN TIMES?

At the head of Egyptian society was the all-powerful pharaoh. He made all the important decisions about how his kingdom was run. **Ministers** helped to rule Egypt, and hundreds of **officials** ran the different regions of the Empire.

POWERFUL PHARAOHS

There were a few examples of powerful female pharaohs, but pharaohs in Ancient Egypt were almost always male. The pharaoh lived in a vast palace with his many wives and children. All the members of the royal family were treated with great respect, but the most important person, after the pharaoh, was his chief wife. The pharaoh usually chose one of his sisters to be his chief wife and her son became the next pharaoh. This way, the divine blood of the pharaohs remained as 'pure' as possible.

As well as ruling their kingdom, pharaohs also led the Egyptian army. One of the greatest warrior pharaohs was Tuthmosis III, who conquered more than 300 cities and led his army to war 17 times over a period of 25 years. Pharaohs gave orders for magnificent monuments to be built. Teams of builders constructed huge pyramids and temples in honour of the pharaohs.

▶ Pharaohs often led their armies in war. In this painting, Pharaoh Ramses II charges into battle, while his enemies fall beneath his chariot.

VIZIERS AND VICEROYS

Three important ministers helped the pharaoh to run Egypt. Two **viziers** were in charge of Upper and Lower Egypt, while a **viceroy** governed Nubia (a large territory to the south of Egypt). These three men had a large staff of officials who collected taxes, ran the law courts, and supervised farming and building projects.

GENERALS AND PRIESTS

Army generals had a lot of power in Ancient Egypt. A few very talented generals even became pharaohs themselves. High priests were also very powerful figures. It was believed that they could interpret the will of the gods, and so they were often asked to advise the pharaoh.

REAL LIVES

TUTANKHAMUN: A BOY PHARAOH

Tutankhamun was the son of Pharaoh Akhenaten. When he was about nine years old, his father died, so Tutankhamun became pharaoh. Around this time he was married to his half-sister Ankhesenamun, who was slightly older than him. Because Tutankhamun was so young, two adult **regents** ruled for him. He died when he was about 19, probably from a broken leg that became infected. Tutankhamun's mummified body was preserved inside a magnificent set of coffin cases, one of which is shown here.

WHAT WAS LIFE LIKE IN AN EGYPTIAN FAMILY?

Most Egyptian families were much larger than families today. An Egyptian household usually consisted of an older married couple and their sons, who each had their own wife and children. Wealthy families also had servants to help them run their home. As well as all these people, there were often animals running around the house: cats, dogs and monkeys were popular family pets.

FAMILY HOMES

Rich Egyptians lived in large villas with many rooms and a central hall for entertaining guests. The rooms were furnished with wooden tables, chairs and beds. Villas often had shady gardens and pools and were sometimes surrounded by their own farming lands.

Ordinary families had simple cottages with just a few rooms. The same room was used for eating and sleeping, and benches around the sides of the room could be used as seats or beds.

▲ Wealthy Egyptian families often lived in villas, surrounded by farmland. This painting shows servants at work in a villa and on its farm.

HUSBANDS AND WIVES

Egyptian girls were usually married in their early teens. Boys often waited to marry until they were around 20 years old and they had become established in their work. Divorce was easy in Egyptian society – both partners had the right to ask the courts to end a marriage. However there is evidence that most couples stayed together for life.

FAMILY SERVANTS

Rich people kept a large staff of servants to help them run their villas and the surrounding lands. Within the home, servants cooked and cleaned and repaired the family's clothes. They also waited on their master and mistress, and helped to care for the children.

▲ A young Egyptian couple from the ruling class. The couple share a carved throne, and they are finely dressed in pleated robes and heavy wigs.

REAL LIVES

MEKET-RE: A VILLA OWNER

Meket-Re was an important Egyptian official who lived in the 3rd century BC. His tomb contains painted wooden models of his family home with its gardens and pool, and also its kitchens, workshops and grain stores. One set of models shows Meket-Re with his son and four scribes, counting the cattle on his estate. The models provide a fascinating picture of the home life of a leading member of the Egyptian ruling class.

BABIES AND YOUNG CHILDREN

In Ancient Egypt, one in five children died before they reached their teens, so people did everything they could to keep them safe. Parents tried to protect their children with prayers and spells, and babies and children wore amulets (lucky charms) around their neck.

Mothers from ordinary families cared for their own children, often breastfeeding them until they were three years old. Wealthy women paid poorer mothers to do the job of breastfeeding their babies.

BOYS AND GIRLS

From an early age, boys and girls were kept apart. Wealthy boys learnt how to read and write. Boys from ordinary families trained to do the same work as their father. A son might work beside his father in the fields, or learn the family trade in a workshop.

Girls of all classes stayed at home with their mothers. Wealthy girls learnt how to run a household and supervise slaves. Girls from poor families were expected to help look after their younger sisters and brothers. They also learnt how to cook and clean, and how to spin and weave cloth to make the family's clothes.

◄ A pharaoh and his teacher. This painting shows a young ruler sitting on the lap of his female tutor. Wealthy Egyptians were often taught at home.

CHILDREN'S TOYS

Young children played with wooden balls, dolls and spinning tops. They also had model animals made from clay or wood. Some of these animals had moving parts that were worked by pulling a string.

▲ Egyptian children played with simple wooden dolls like this. The doll is painted with colourful designs and has mud beads for hair.

REAL LIVES

"SHERIT": A MUCH-LOVED CHILD

Archaeologists have recently examined the **mummy** of a young Egyptian girl. They discovered that she had long curly hair and was between four and six years old. They also found she had been breast fed until about a year before she died. No expense had been spared on the little girl's funeral. She wore a golden face mask, and her body had been carefully prepared for burial – almost certainly by her loving parents. The girl's body shows no sign of injury, so she may have died from an infectious disease or from food poisoning (both very common causes of death). Her real name is not known, but archaeologists have called her Sherit, an Egyptian name that means "little one".

DID EGYPTIAN CHILDREN GO TO SCHOOL?

Most Egyptian children did not go to school. Children in poor families had to help their parents with their work, and rich boys and girls often had a private tutor to teach them at home. However, there were some schools attached to the temples, although they only took boys.

TEMPLE SCHOOLS

Some temple schools were attached to important temples in the cities, and only took boys from the ruling classes. There were also smaller temple schools in the villages. The village schools were open to all boys, but they were expensive so families had to save up to send their sons to school.

Boys started at temple school when they were around five years old. For the first few years, they concentrated on copying texts and reading aloud. The teachers at the temple schools were very strict and pupils were often beaten for not working hard enough.

Older pupils studied more advanced texts, such as the *Book of Wisdom*, which gave advice to young men on how to behave. Later, some students specialized in different subjects such as mathematics, religion, engineering or medicine.

▲ The Ancient Egyptians did not have an alphabet. Instead, they used a system of picture signs – known as **hieroglyphs** - to write things down. The hieroglyphs shown here were painted on a coffin.

EGYPTIAN WRITING

Egyptian writing was very hard to learn because it was made up of more than 700 picture signs called hieroglyphs. Some of the hieroglyphs represent an object or a person. Others represent a sound.

School pupils wrote with a reed pen dipped in ink. They practised their writing on pieces of broken pottery or flakes of stone that could be thrown away. By the end of their schooling, they were ready to write on **papyrus** – a kind of fine white paper made from reeds.

SCRIBES

Many pupils at temple schools later became **scribes**. This was a very important job, and scribes had a high position in Egyptian society. They kept all the records needed to run the kingdom of Egypt. They also wrote the histories of the pharaohs and their deeds.

▼ A carving of the scribe Amenhotep at work. Amenhotep sits cross-legged to write on his scroll, using his stretched-out kilt as a desk.

REAL LIVES

AMENHOTEP: A ROYAL SCRIBE

Amenhotep was a very well educated man. He was the special scribe of Pharaoh Amenhotep III, but also an architect, priest, teacher and healer. He drew out the plans for the pharaoh's massive building projects and organized their construction. After his death, he became famous for his teachings. Amenhotep was eventually worshipped as a god of healing.

WHAT JOBS DID EGYPTIAN PEOPLE DO?

Most Egyptians were farmers on the banks of the River Nile. Many others worked as fishermen, weavers or potters. Educated people had jobs as government officials, priests, scribes and doctors. Merchants made long journeys to exchange goods, and men of all classes joined the army.

WOMEN'S WORK

Most Egyptian women stayed at home, but a few had careers. Noblewomen could become priestesses. They could also work as singers, dancers and musicians in the temples. Poorer women had jobs as weavers in workshops, or as servants to the rich. Women from farming families worked with the men in the fields.

▼ Egyptian couples often worked together in the fields. Here, the husband ploughs the earth and scares away the birds, while his wife follows, sowing seeds.

SLAVE LABOUR

By the time of the New Kingdom, slavery was common. Many slaves were prisoners-of-war from the lands that the Egyptians had won for their Empire (see pages 6-7). They were often employed as builders, miners, or household servants. Some slaves had very hard lives, but others were well treated. A few slaves were set free and some of them married local people.

WORKING ON THE LAND

Egyptian farmers grew a range of vegetables, figs, dates and grapes but their main crop was wheat. Most of the land was used for crops, but farmers also kept some animals, such as sheep, pigs, goats, geese and ducks. Oxen were used as working animals, and only rich farmers reared cows to eat.

CRAFT WORKERS

Skilled Egyptian craft workers produced a wide range of goods. Potters worked with clay, or carved pots from stone, and carpenters used local and imported woods to make furniture and statues. Metalworkers made tools and weapons, and jewellers created elaborate pieces from silver and gold, beads and precious stones. Craft workers sometimes worked in a family group, or as part of a team in a large workshop.

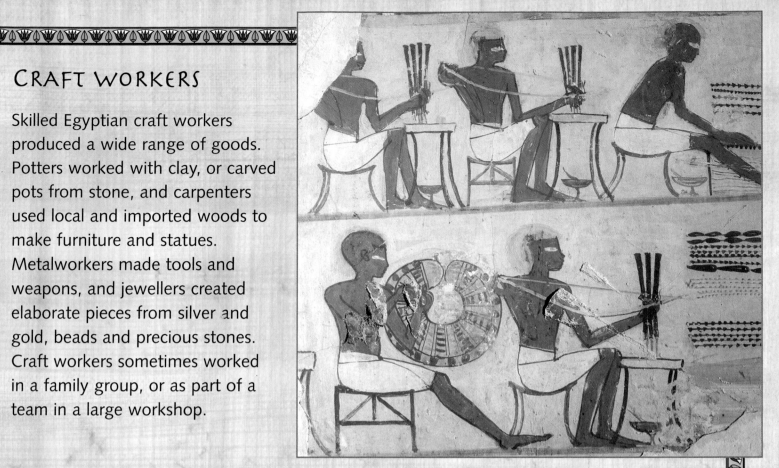

▲ This painting shows a jewellery workshop. The workers are boring holes in beads, polishing the beads, and threading them onto a wide collar.

REAL LIVES

ASRU: A SINGER

A coffin has survived from Ancient Egypt containing the mummified body of a working woman. The coffin **inscription** says that she was Asru, a singer in a temple. Archaeologists believe Asru was at least 60 when she died. This was unusual in Egyptian times, when most women did not survive beyond 40. Asru's long life was probably due to the fact that she had a safe and comfortable life working in a temple.

Building temples and pyramids

Thousands of Egyptians worked on the massive pyramids and temples of Ancient Egypt. Miners cut stone from quarries, while stonecutters shaped it into blocks. Then teams of workers hauled the blocks onto sledges and took them to where they were needed. Builders set the massive stones in place and masons trimmed them to fit.

Army life

By the time of the New Kingdom, Egypt had a large professional army. The ordinary soldiers came from the lower classes, but officers were always educated, wealthy men. Life in the Egyptian army was tough. Soldiers were sent on long marches and had to train very hard. Egyptian soldiers carried spears and shields, but they had no protective armour so they suffered terrible injuries.

Doctors

Egyptian doctors were famous throughout the Middle East for their skill. They studied medical texts and specialized in different areas of the body, such as the stomach, the teeth or the head. Doctors performed surgery, sewed up cuts, set broken limbs and treated wounds. They also made medicines from plants and **minerals** and even animal parts. If these methods failed to work, doctors also tried to use spells and magic charms to help them cure their patients.

▼ This painting shows workmen pulling blocks of stone on a sledge. The man at the back of the group is probably the foreman, who gave orders to the workers.

An embalmer prepares a body for burial. The embalmer wears a mask carved with the head of Anubis, the god of the dead.

EMBALMERS

The Egyptians believed in life after death. They thought that the dead would need their bodies in the **next world**, so they preserved the bodies as **mummies**. The people who did this important work were known as **embalmers**. They worked in tents beside the River Nile.

Embalmers prepared the bodies of the dead for burial. First, they removed the brains and **internal organs** and stored them in jars. Then they covered the body with a salt called natron to help it dry out. When the body was thoroughly dry, its insides were stuffed with a mixture of linen, sawdust, and sweet-smelling spices. Finally, the embalmers wrapped the mummy in layers of bandages, and placed it in a coffin, ready to be buried in a tomb.

REAL LIVES

IMHOTEP: A MAN WITH MANY JOBS

Imhotep was the architect of Egypt's first pyramid, which was built for Pharaoh Djoser. He was also the **chancellor** of Egypt, and ran the kingdom's finances. However these were not his only jobs. Imhotep also worked as a **high priest**, a sculptor, and a doctor!

WHAT DID EGYPTIAN ADULTS AND CHILDREN WEAR?

In the hot, dry climate of Ancient Egypt people did not need many clothes. In fact, most children went naked until they were in their teens. Most Egyptians wore simple clothes, but added a lot of jewellery to make themselves look good.

▲ Most Egyptians dressed very simply, in kilts for the men and long tunic-dresses for the women. Women's tunics were usually white, but sometimes they were dyed dramatic colours.

CHANGING STYLES

Until the time of the New Kingdom, all the Egyptians wore the same basic clothes. Men wore a simple kilt, made from a piece of linen wrapped around the waist. Women wore a long tunic that reached to their ankles. Wealthy people's clothes were made from fine linen, while ordinary people used a thicker, coarser cloth. People of all classes wore sandals made from reeds.

In the New Kingdom, styles changed. Fashionable people wore cloaks made from very thin, pleated linen. Some men wore a double kilt (one long and one short) and women's tunics were decorated with ornaments and fringes.

LOOKING GOOD

Rich men and women spent a lot of time on their looks. They bathed every day and rubbed scented oils on their skin. Both sexes wore heavy eye make-up. They believed that it protected their eyes from the glare of the sun and prevented eye disease. For special occasions, men and women wore heavy wigs, decorated with beads and jewels.

All Egyptians liked to wear jewellery, and both men and women wore necklaces, bracelets and earrings. Wealthy people wore jewellery made from gold and precious stones. Poor people's jewellery was made from copper and beads.

▶ A carving of the elegant Queen Nefertiti. Here, the queen wears a simple crown and a wide bead necklace.

A SPECIAL HAIRSTYLE

Egyptian children had their own special hairstyle. Their hair was shaved off or kept very short except for a lock on the side of the head. This long, s-shaped curl was called the "side-lock of youth". Children wore this style until they were around 12 years old, when they were considered to be adults.

REAL LIVES

NEFERTITI: A BEAUTIFUL QUEEN

Nefertiti was the chief wife of Pharaoh Akhaten and the mother of six daughters. In carvings, she is shown as very beautiful, with a long, slim neck and carefully made-up eyes and lips. Some carvers show her standing beside the pharaoh as his equal, and this probably means she had great influence over her husband.

HOW DID EGYPTIAN ADULTS AND CHILDREN HAVE FUN?

People in Ancient Egypt really liked to enjoy themselves. Wealthy Egyptians held lavish banquets, with music and dancing. Kings and nobles hunted for sport, and people of all classes played sports and games.

EGYPTIAN PARTIES

Rich Egyptians held large parties. They provided banquets with many courses and laid on plenty of entertainments. During the feast, musicians played on harps, flutes, pipes and drums. Later in the evening, singers, dancers, jugglers and acrobats entertained the guests.

HUNTING AND FISHING

Hunting and fishing were popular sports for wealthy Egyptians. Nobles hunted water birds on the banks of the Nile, or rode on chariots into the desert to hunt for lions, ostriches and cobras. Sometimes hunters formed a team to spear a hippo and catch it in a net. Other noblemen preferred to stay at home, and fish in their own garden pools.

▶ In this painting of a banquet, servant girls dance for the guests and serve them food. Servants also placed cones of perfumed fat on the guests' heads. The cones gradually melted, creating a sweet smell.

Sport and games

The Egyptians loved to compete against each other in athletic contests. Ancient Egyptian sports included boxing, gymnastics, running, rowing, jumping, and throwing the javelin. People played a kind of hockey, using palm tree branches for sticks and a leather ball stuffed with papyrus. They also formed teams for energetic tugs-of-war, in which each team pulled as hard as they could to show they were the strongest.

When they were not playing sports, Egyptians of all ages liked to relax at home with a board game. One of the most popular games was 'senet'. It had a set of pieces that were moved across a board, rather like the modern game of backgammon.

REAL LIVES

NEBAMUN: A NOBLE WHO LOVED TO HUNT

Nebamun was a nobleman who died around 1400 BC. In a painting in his tomb (shown here) he is seen hunting for birds in the marshes of the River Nile. Nebamun is shown holding a throwing stick, which was used to stun the birds. Also in the painting are his wife and daughter and his handsome ginger cat. Nebamun's cat would have been specially trained to frighten the birds from their hiding place.

How important was religion for the Egyptians?

The Ancient Egyptians worshipped dozens of gods and goddesses. Every village had its own shrine, where people could say prayers and leave offerings to the gods. There were also massive temples on the banks of the Nile. On feast days, priests carried statues of the gods around towns and cities, while people sang songs and prayed. Then the priests **sacrificed** animals to the gods.

▲ This carving shows a man presenting an offering to a sacred bull. Behind the bull stands the goddess Isis.

Talking to the gods

Everybody in Ancient Egypt tried to follow the will of the gods. If they had to make a big decision in their lives, they paid a scribe to write down their question for the god. This request was handed to a priest who disappeared into the temple and returned with an answer. Then the grateful people left a gift of thanks to the gods.

Preparing for the Next World

The Egyptians believed that, after they died, they would go to the next world to live with the gods. This belief led them to bury the dead with great care (see page 21). Embalmers preserved the bodies of people of all classes and even favourite pets. People were often buried with their possessions, so that they would have everything they needed in the next world.

SERVANTS OF THE GODS

Some men and women devoted their lives to the gods. Women often worked as musicians and dancers in the temples. Male priests conducted ceremonies and wrote sacred texts. Some priests and priestesses worked in large temples, which contained a statue of a god or goddess. Every morning, they 'woke' the statue. Then they washed and dressed it, offered it food and prayed to it.

▶ Pharaoh Ramses II built two magnificent temples at Abu Simbel in honour of the gods. These four giant figures carved from the rock represent Ramses and three other gods.

REAL LIVES

THUYA: A PRIESTESS

Thuya was the **high priestess** of the rain god Min. She was married to Yuya, the high priest of Min. The couple were important people at the court of Pharaoh Amenhotep III. (Yuya was in charge of the royal chariots.) Later, their daughter Tiy became Queen of Egypt. Thuya's golden mummy case shows a round-faced woman with a very contented smile.

GLOSSARY

archaeologist Someone who learns about the past by examining old buildings and objects.

chancellor The person in charge of a country's money.

civilization A well-organized society.

dynasty A ruling family.

embalmer Someone who prepares the bodies of the dead for burial.

fertile Good for growing crops.

general A leader of soldiers in an army.

hieroglyph A picture or a symbol that represents an object, a letter, or a sound.

high priest/ priestess A very important man/woman priest.

inscription A carved message, often on a tomb.

internal organs Body parts, such as the heart or the stomach, that are on the inside of the body.

irrigate To supply water to crops.

mineral A substance, such as iron and salt, which is found under the earth.

minister Someone in charge of a government department.

mummy A body that has been specially treated and then wrapped in bandages, to stop it from decaying.

next world A place where the dead go after their life on earth, according to Ancient Egyptian beliefs.

official Someone who holds an important position in a government.

papyrus A kind of paper made from a reed-like plant.

pharaoh An Egyptian king.

regent Someone who rules on behalf of the real ruler of a country.

sacrifice To kill an animal and offer it as a gift to a god.

scribe Someone who copies out letters and other documents by hand.

viceroy Someone who acts as a deputy to a ruler, taking charge of part of their land. A viceroy governed Nubia, a territory to the south of Ancient Egypt.

vizier Someone who acts as a deputy to a ruler, taking charge of part of their land. Two viziers governed Upper and Lower Egypt.

Further Information

More books to read

George Hart
Ancient Egypt
(Dorling Kindersley, 1990)

Gill Harvey and Struan Reid
**The Usborne Encylopedia
of Ancient Egypt**
(Usborne, 2001)

Fiona Macdonald
Women in Ancient Egypt
(Belitha Press, 1999)

John Malam
Ancient Egyptian Jobs
(Heinemann Library, 2002)

Stewart Ross
**Find Out About: Ancient
Egypt**
(Hodder Wayland, 2006)

Useful websites

http://www.ancientegypt.co.uk/menu.html
A very well illustrated site from the British Museum,
including sections on pharaohs and trades.

http://www.iwebquest.com/egypt/ancientegypt.htm
A well-organized site for children, with lots of projects.

http://www.mnsu.edu/emuseum/prehistory/egypt/
A large site including sections on daily life, religion,
history and art.

http://www.egyptologyonline.com/introduction.htm
A well-illustrated site, with sections on many different
aspects of life in Ancient Egypt.

Places to visit

The British Museum, London, UK
A very large collection of mummies,
coffins and carvings

The Pitt-Rivers Museum, Oxford, UK
Several interesting mummies, including
some mummified cats

The Egyptian Museum, Cairo, Egypt
The best collection in the world of
treasures excavated from Ancient
Egyptian tombs, including the golden
mummies of Tutankhamun

**The Metropolitan Museum
New York, USA**
A large collection of Ancient Egyptian
objects, including carvings, jewellery
and tomb models

INDEX

Numbers in **bold** indicate pictures.

Alexander the Great 7
amulets 14
animals 12, 18, 24
archaeologists 15, 19
army 10, **10**, 18, 20

babies 14
banquets **24**
breastfeeding 14, 15
building projects 11, 17

chancellor 21
children 8, 9, **9**, 10, 12, 13, 14, 15, **15**, 16, 22, 23
civilization 6
cleaning 13, 15
Cleopatra 7, **7**
clothes 13, 15, 22, **22**
cooking 13, 15
craft workers 19, **19**

divorce 13
doctors 20, 21

embalmers 21, **21**, 26

farming 11, 12, 18, **18**
funeral 15
furniture 12

games 24, 25
gardens 12, 13
goddesses **8**, 26, **26**
gods 10, 11, 17, 26, 27

hair styles 23
hieroglyphs **16**, 17
high priests 11, 21, 27

jewellery **19**, 22, 23
jobs 8, 14, 18, **18**, 19, **19**, 20, **20**, 21, **21**

make-up 22
marriage 9, 12, 13, 18
medicines 20
men 8, **9**, **13**, 18, **18**, **20**, 22, **22**, 25, 26
Middle Kingdom 6, 7
mummies 15, 21

natron 21
New Kingdom 6, 7, 18, 20, 22

Old Kingdom 6, 7

papyrus 17
pets 12, 26
pharaohs 6, **8**, 10, **10**, 11, **11**, 17, 21, 23, **27**
poor people 8, 9, 15, 16, 18, 23

priestesses 18
pyramids 6, 10, 20

River Euphrates 6
River Nile 6, 18, 21, 25, 26

schools 16, 17
scribes 13, 17, **17**, 18, 26
servants 8, **12**, 13, 15, **24**
shrines 26
slavery 18
sports 24, 25, **25**

temples 10, 16, 18, 19, 20, 27, **27**
toys 15, **15**
tutors **14**, 16

viceroy 11
villas 12, **12**, 13
viziers 11

wealthy people 8, 9, 12, 14, 15, 16, 18, 20, 22, 23, 24
women 8, **9**, **13**, 15, 18 **18**, 22, **22**, 27
writing 17